Query
Caboodle

Query
Caboodle

Heller Levinson

BLACK
WIDOW
PRESS

Boston, MA

Black Widow Press is an imprint of Commonwealth Books,
Inc., Boston, MA. Distributed to the trade by NBN (National
Book Network) throughout North America, Canada, and the U.K.
All Black Widow Press books are printed on acid-free paper, and
glued into bindings. Black Widow Press and its logo are registered
trademarks of Commonwealth Books, Inc.

Joseph S. Phillips and Susan J. Wood, Ph.D., Publishers
www.blackwidowpress.com

Cover design: Linda Lynch
Layout: Kerrie Kemperman
Cover art: Linda Lynch, *Prow Drawing I (to A.P. Ryder)*,
pastel pigment on cotton paper, detail, 22^1/4 x 30 inches, 2021

ISBN-13: 979-8-9880852-1-8
Printed in the United States
10 9 8 7 6 5 4 3 2 1

Nothing should be decided but should be put in question.

how much of hinges

The 'how much of' modules developed to densify the particle (the subject matter). As they cropped up in various applications, I noted their luminous nature when stood-apart, highlit by their own provocations.

I considered how much of 'how much of's' appeal was due to its traditional usage as a quantitative query, now reoriented to release metaphysical posits.

In this Hinge Capacity, 'how much of' moves toward *consideration* rather than *conclusion*.

The 'where in' module shares the 'how much of' inclination to subvert the quantitative impulse & replace it with the Querulous, with the eminences accruing from *dislodge*. The urge is *probe* not formulation.

Additional modules are continuously in development.

how much of

lost

is

find

how much of

find

is

transparent

how much of

lost

is

privilege

how much of

saunter

is

rooted

how much of

education

begs

the question

how much of

tremolo

is

forgiveness

how much of

tremolo

begs the question

how much of

leverage

is

unbalanced

how much of

sinew

is

tenuous

how much of

intrigue

is

supposition

how much of

love

is

irremediable

how much of

learning

is

pre-heated

how much of

aura

is

evaporation

how much of

astray

g   r

                         a

                 z

e

                 s

how much of

occlusion

is

remiss

Why does talking to trees make so much sense?

where in

subtraction

is the

additional

where in the

additional

is

abundance

how much of

abundance

is

courting

where in the

gather

is

ravel

how much of

ravel

is

unruly

where in

breakage

is

assurance

how much of

division

is

discretion

how much of

calculation

abrades

where in the

alone

is

orthodox

where in the

wander

is

steadfast

if there is not one correct answer, are questions valid?

if there is no one 'right' answer, & only questions, then

there is no answer. only provisional solutions.

a solution is not an answer. it is an efficacy.

where in

steadfast

is

oscillate

where in the

embark

is

reclamation

where in the

query

is

resolution

how much of

resolution

resolves

where in the

resolve

is

steadfast

how much of

steadfast

is

steady

where in the

query

is

saunter

Is the Human the animal with the most devisements?

Would there be the Human without the hand?

How much handicraft is in the hand?

how much of

calibration

neglects

where in

neglect

is

follow-through

how much of

deplete

is

overlooked

where in

prosperity

is

richness

where in

paucity

is

surplus

where in the

margin

is

fibrillation?

adjacency?

compromise?

how much of

shift

is

shifty

how much of

edge

is

contour

where in the

edge

is the

swivel

where in the

swivel

is

motion

how much of

love

is

concatenation

where in the

collection

is

deposit

where in the

loaf

is the

eke-out

where in the

presentation

is

evacuation

how much of

appetite

is

colorless

how much of

appetite

is

supply-side reactive

how much of

surmise

is

postulate

where in the

innate

is

design

how much of

leer

is

enterprise

where in the

unravel

is

mitigation

how much of

restless

is

unnecessary

how much of

gist

is

gustatory

where in the

render

is

fabulation

where in the

abyss

is

lurk

how much of

lure

transpires

where in

desperation

is

free-for-all

how much of

lickety-split

is

secondary

when asked why do you like something, e.g., the trombone, is it sufficient to say 'because I do.'

are we providing a more fulfilling response if we cite the trombone's attractions, e.g., its lungy tone, the shape of the bell, the sexiness of the slide?

does listing attributes come up empty? fail to deliver the whole truth?

when asked why do you love someone, what is the whole truth?

where in

whereabouts

is

what for

where in

whereabouts

is

wonder

where in

departure

is

augment

where in

acquisition

is

augment

how much of

calculation

diminishes

how much of

equation

is

inequitable

how much of

the uncountable

is a

superior mathematics

where in the

appearing

is

sustain

how much of

what you tell yourself

is

all there is

how much of

experience

is

relevant

how much of

technology

is

encroachment

where in the

human

is

identification

how much of

containment

exacerbates

how much of

containment

is

comfort.

Why does someone receive congratulations for a new acquisition? a new home, a watch, a car?

Is there a victory involved?

how much of

linger

exacerbates

where in

abode

is

akin

what about Snow produces Smiles

how much of

the cloud

is

cloudy

whereabouts is where

how much of

'passage'

misleads

how much of

be wilder

is

bewildering

where in

bewilder

is

be wild

how much of

irrelevancy

counts

where in

consider

is

consideration

how much of

acumen

is

agitation

do truisms run true

how much of

adaptation

is

accommodation

how much of

inconvenience

self-administrates

how much of

indecision

is

wisdom

how much of

transparency

occludes

how much of

agility

is

surprise

how much of

foreplay

is

inconsequential

how much of

learning

is

misrepresentation

how much of

compromise

is

compression

how much of

bewilder

begs the question

.

how much of

elucidation

disintegrates

where in the

numerical

is the

questionable

how much of

quarantine

is

escapism

how much of

you

is

yourself

how much of

wisdom

is

accumulation

how much of

industrious

is

affirmation

how much of

will

is

unaccountable

where in the

empty

is

navigation

how much of

empty

is

navigable

how much of

empty

is

climactic

how much of

empty

is

identifiable

where in the

quatrain

is

estimable

fasten/fascination: does fascination entail fastenment

does fastenment result in fascination

how much of

empty

is

unrecognizable

where in the

empty

is

consultation

. does white carry a pride other colors don't?

. is something pulled from context reborn?

. does regularity breed constipation?

how much of

love

is

accidental

how much of

accidental

is

habit forming

how much of

empty

is

irregular

WIND

does wind wind-up?

amass its forces before the unleash?

'Wind is air in motion. It is caused by uneven
heating of the atmosphere by energy from the sun.'

> *disturbance*
>
> how much of
>
> disturbance
>
> is
>
> formative?
>
> is
>
> havoc?

Paul Blackburn: *I am a wind on the deep waters*   .

The wind that drives the floods   .

Beryl sea-green is the stone   .

Dwelling secure in the hollow

ship until

wind wafts him home

Clear is the color of the wind in the

               aspen (white

                     poplar)

is the wind weedless?

       wordless?

syllables contralto mush lullaby lyre the

wind, footprint the sun

                    where in the

                    wind

                    is

                    embark

              bellows/

                  nautical/

                     ahoy

Charles Olson: *It was the west wind caught her up, as*

        she rose

        from the genital

wave, and bore her from the delicate

foam, home

to her isle

wind irruptive, contemplator of measures

Wind travels because of air pressure.

Does placidity nullify the excursion?

     'The calm belt of air near the equator is called

the *doldrums*.'

What is the difference between breeze & wind?

is breeze Mozart & wind Wagner?

         or

breeze = Morandi   wind = Van Gogh?

a hop, skip, & a jump to

windfall

Why do so many of the newly retired take up painting?

where in

monetization

is

empathy

how much of

the

unremarkable

is

remarkable

how much of

community

is

commonality

how much of

place

is

misplaced

how much of

place

is

geography?

preoccupation?

outlook?

inlook?

how much of

travel

is

spatial corruption

how much of

approach

demurs

arrival

These lines from Clayton Eshleman's Introduction to
FRACTURE have always enamored:

> There are only a handful of primary incidents in
> one's life, incidents powerful enough to create
> the cracks or boundary lines that one will often
> enter and follow for many years before another
> crucial event pounds one deeper or reorients one
> to a new map. As one approaches these events,
> omens appear everywhere, the world becomes
> dangerously magical, as if one had called the
> gods and the gods were now answering.

Then, after emailing the above to a colleague &
receiving an "absolutely love this" by way of response,
I was triggered to query the passage more deeply.
Query Caboodle was conditioning me to question my
own 'attachments.'

I replied:

Me too (loving it), that's why I sent it. It's magical.
Although now I'm viewing it differently. Or, at least
querying: such as, rather than a 'handful,' if one is pay-
ing attention, *heeding* one's life, there might be con-
tinuous daily adjustments. A profusion of such

profound 'orientating' that the so-called primary would no longer be 'primary' but merely 'incidental' to fluid evolution, — *absorbed into* the primary movement stream, into the Vastness, whereby 'incidentals' would be just that, . . . incidental to Monumental Motility.

Simply thinking about this, — trying to see options, looking differently.

ABSORB

soak

    scoop upinto

bibulous endosomotic imbibe

    draw

porosity-dependent the in-swell

courts the aperture, ink-

    lings passage, plots admix, flesh—

out reliquarian seduction rouse,

    infiltrate

    in-amass-take

    constitute

S Although ABSORB is not formally formulated as a query function it functions as such in that its 'identity' — the full manifestation of its character, its Being-hood — is being probed. In this sense, all Term applications share the querulous.

how much of

caliber

is

immeasurable

where in the

curve

is the

straightaway

what is knowing?

is it a move toward discipline?

toward encounter?

is there knowledge without encounter?

how many types of encounter can we count?

can we count on encounter counting?

how much of

knowing

is

instinctual?

institutional?

predicated?

averted?

where in the

affliction

is

indulgence

how much of

volition

is

agitation

how much of

assumption

is

presumption

how much of

diatribe

is

forsaken

how much of painting

depends upon a wall?

how much of

reminiscence

is

lame

Has any animal exalted the regimen of food to the extreme the human has?

how much of

consideration

is

ill-advised

how much of

ill-advisement

is

inconsiderate

how much of

linger

is

luster

how much of

luster

is

linger

how much of

learning

is

misrepresentation

how much of

un-learning

is

learned

how much of

repair

is

judgmental

how much of

absorb

is

inchoate

how much of

remission

is

suggestive

where in

delinquency

is

navigation

how much of

navigable

is

disputable

how much of

query

begs the question

The originator of Hinge Theory, HELLER LEVINSON lives in New York.

BLACK WIDOW PRESS :: POETRY IN TRANSLATION

BLACK WIDOW PRESS :: MODERN POETRY SERIES

RALPH ADAMO
All the Good Hiding Places: Poems

WILLIS BARNSTONE
ABC of Translation
African Bestiary (forthcoming)

DAVE BRINKS
The Caveat Onus
The Secret Brain: Selected Poems 1995–2012

RUXANDRA CESEREANU
California (on the Someş). Translated by
    Adam J. Sorkin and Ruxandra Cesereanu.
Crusader-Woman. Translated by Adam J. Sorkin.
    Introduction by Andrei Codrescu.
Forgiven Submarine by Ruxandra Cesereanu
    and Andrei Codrescu.

ANDREI CODRESCU
Forgiven Submarine by Ruxandra Cesereanu
    and Andrei Codrescu.
Too Late for Nightmares: Poems

CLAYTON ESHLEMAN
An Alchemist with One Eye on Fire
Anticline
Archaic Design
Clayton Eshleman/The Essential Poetry: 1960–2015
Grindstone of Rapport: A Clayton Eshleman Reader
Penetralia
Pollen Aria
The Price of Experience
Endure: Poems by Bei Dao. Translated by Clayton
    Eshleman and Lucas Klein.
Curdled Skulls: Poems of Bernard Bador.
    Translated by Bernard Bador with Clayton Eshleman.

PIERRE JORIS
Barzakh (Poems 2000–2012)
Exile Is My Trade: A Habib Tengour Reader

MARILYN KALLET
Even When We Sleep
How Our Bodies Learned
Packing Light: New and Selected Poems
The Love That Moves Me
Disenchanted City (La ville désenchantée)
    by Chantal Bizzini. Translated by J. Bradford
    Anderson, Darren Jackson, and Marilyn Kallet.

ROBERT KELLY
Fire Exit
The Hexagon

STEPHEN KESSLER
Garage Elegies
Last Call

BILL LAVENDER
Memory Wing

HELLER LEVINSON
from stone this running
jus' sayn'
LinguaQuake
Lure
Lurk
Query Caboodle
Seep
Shift Gristle
Tenebraed
Un-
Wrack Lariat

JOHN OLSON
Backscatter: New and Selected Poems
Dada Budapest
Larynx Galaxy
Weave of the Dream King

NIYI OSUNDARE
City Without People: The Katrina Poems
Green: Sighs of Our Ailing Planet: Poems

MEBANE ROBERTSON
An American Unconscious
Signal from Draco: New and Selected Poems

JEROME ROTHENBERG
Concealments and Caprichos
Eye of Witness: A Jerome Rothenberg Reader.
    Edited with commentaries by Heriberto Yepez &
    Jerome Rothenberg.
The President of Desolation & Other Poems

AMINA SAÏD
The Present Tense of the World: Poems 2000–2009.
Translated with an introduction by Marilyn Hacker.

JULIAN SEMILIAN
Osiris with a trombone across the seam of insubstance

ANIS SHIVANI
Soraya (Sonnets)

JERRY W. WARD, JR.
Fractal Song

BLACK WIDOW PRESS :: ANTHOLOGIES / BIOGRAPHIES

*Barbaric Vast & Wild: A Gathering of Outside and
Subterranean Poetry (Poems for the Millennium,* vol.
5). Jerome Rothenberg and John Bloomberg-Rissman,
editors.

Clayton Eshleman: The Whole Art by Stuart Kendall

Revolution of the Mind: The Life of André Breton
by Mark Polizzotti